Rap Your World

RAPPING Rhymes about School

Thomas Kingsley Troupe

BLACK
RABBIT
BOOKS

Hi Jinx is published by Black Rabbit Books
P.O. Box 3263, Mankato, Minnesota, 56002.
www.blackrabbitbooks.com
Copyright © 2021 Black Rabbit Books

Jen Besel, editor; Michael Sellner, designer;
Omay Ayres, photo researcher

Library of Congress Cataloging-in-Publication Data
Names: Troupe, Thomas Kingsley, author.
Title: Rapping rhymes about school /
by Thomas Kingsley Troupe.
Description: Mankato, Minnesota : Black Rabbit
Books, [2021] | Series: Hi jinx. Rap your world |
Includes bibliographical references. |
Audience: Ages 8-12. | Audience: Grades 4-6. |
Summary: Examines the world of school through
poems meant for rapping. Includes suggestions
for creating raps about school.
Identifiers: LCCN 2019026961 (print) |
LCCN 2019026962 (ebook) |
ISBN 9781623103224 (hardcover) |
ISBN 9781644664186 (paperback) |
ISBN 9781623104160 (ebook) |
Subjects: LCSH: Schools—Juvenile poetry. |
Children's poetry, American. | CYAC: Schools—Poetry. |
American poetry.
Classification: LCC PS3620.R6825 R38 2021 (print) |
LCC PS3620.R6825 (ebook) | DDC 811/.6—dc23
LC record available at https://lccn.loc.gov/2019026961
LC ebook record available at https://lccn.loc.gov/2019026962

Printed in the United States. 1/20

Image Credits

Alamy: Daniel Cole, 13, 18; Foss, 14; Janpen Chaiyadej, 10–11;
iStock: Adelevin, 4–5; Big_Ryan, 2–3; ChrisGorgio, 14–15;
denis_pc, 6–7; kbeis, 10–11; Sybirko, 20; zaricm, 13; Shutterstock:
ADudkov, 3, 21; alexmstudio, 8; AmazeinDesign, Cover, 4–5,
21; Apolinarias, 14–15; Arcady, 1; Christopher Hall, Cover, 3,
4–5, 7, 8, 11, 12, 15, 16, 19; Dmitry Natashin, 16; ekler, 12;
GraphicMama, 9; GraphicsRF, 13, 20; mejnak, 19; Memo Angeles,
1, 16–17, 18–19, 23; mohinimurti, 17; opicobello, 11, 14–15;
Pasko Maksim, 9, 23, 24; pitju, 5, 21; Ron Dale, 5, 8, 12, 18, 20;
Sergey Bogdanov, Cover; STREET STYLE, Cover, 1, 4; studiostoks,
Cover, 4; totallypic, 9, 20; Tueris, Cover, 1, 16; vectorpouch, 13;
Vectors bySkop, 8; Verzzh, 14–15; Visual Generation, 16–17; your,
8; Every effort has been made to contact copyright holders for
material reproduced in this book. Any omissions will be rectified in
subsequent printings if notice is given to the publisher.

Contents

4

Chapter 1

Rap Your World!

Hey! Callin' all rappers! Do you like to rhyme, maybe spin **turntables**, or drop beats in time? The best stuff to rhyme is the stuff that you know, And going to school — *you know about that show.*

Hey, school is the place where you're filled up with smarts,
Like math, writing, science, and some **creative arts**.
Classmates and tests, plus those lockers and books,
And the school cafeteria is always filled with good cooks.

In school, Mrs. Leahy was my favorite teacher,
Had me reading all the time, like a book-reading creature.
All those subjects we learned, yo, to sharpen our skill,
Like how to add and read and write and do a fire drill.

Chapter 2

School Days

The school morning is here, so back to bed you can't flop,

Eat your breakfast, brush your teeth, and hit the bus stop.

Riding the bus in style—that's how we get to school,

Miss a day of learning? Yo, that sounds so **cruel**.

Your locker's a metal closet where you put all your things.

So stuff it all in there before the bell rings.

Your bag and your books, maybe even your ball,

Lock it up, head to class, but don't run down the hall.

Your teacher is instructing and up there running the class.

If you need to use the bathroom, you'll have to get a hall pass.

Listen up and pay attention to the words that they speak,

You'll need to know it for the test you'll take next week.

Your classmates are nearby or just across the aisle,
Like Ruby, Brian, Jenny, and some new kid named Kyle.
When your teacher is teachin', it's no time for squawking,
You don't want to get yourself in big trouble for talking.

Chapter 3

School Subjects

When it comes to numbers, yo, you gotta be exact.

Math is where you learn to multiply, add, or subtract.

Science is the subject where you learn about things,

Like the human body and why tree stumps have rings.

The gymnasium is a classroom of a different size,

Where you learn fun new activities and exercise.

The media center is full of good books for reading,

To fill your brain with knowledge that you know it's needing.

Each year, trees grow. The new growth forms in a circle and looks like a ring.

Yo, here's another subject I always found exciting,

Putting words together, I'm talking about writing.

The more we practice writing, the quicker we'll get better,

At making a note, creating a rap, or writing a letter.

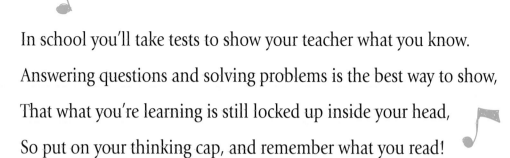

In school you'll take tests to show your teacher what you know.

Answering questions and solving problems is the best way to show,

That what you're learning is still locked up inside your head,

So put on your thinking cap, and remember what you read!

The world's oldest school is in Morocco. It was started in the year 859.

In art class we learn about artists to celebrate,

They **inspire** our own art—it's amazing to create.

Ever wonder about the beats and the rhymes that I kick?
In school we had a class where we studied music!

Some studies say schools with music programs have an **estimated** 90 percent **graduation rate**. In schools without programs, about 73 percent of students graduate.

Chapter 4

Taking a Break

You've been in hard classes, and your mind is just beat,

Let's hit the cafeteria, y'all. It's now time to eat!

Bring your lunch box or eat food from the school,

There's plenty of healthy stuff—no need to drool.

Studying and learning can leave your brain in pieces,

So take a break and head outside for some time at recess.

Catching up and playing games out on the playground,

You'll know your time is up when you hear the bell sound!

Some scientists say kids who get longer recesses do better in school.

Chapter 5
Get in on the Hi Jinx

Just itching to bust a rhyme? Make a rap about school! First, find words that remind you about school. Next, find words that rhyme with the ones on your list. Make those matching words the ends of your lines. Turn them into sentences that make sense and BAM! You've started a rap.

Take It One Step More

1. Did you read the lines to a beat? If you didn't, tap your hand on your leg in a steady rhythm. Try reading the words in time to the beat. How does that change your understanding of the information?

2. Rapping is a form of musical poetry. Is rapping a good way to learn information?

3. Have someone else read the raps out loud. Do they put **accents** in the same places you do?

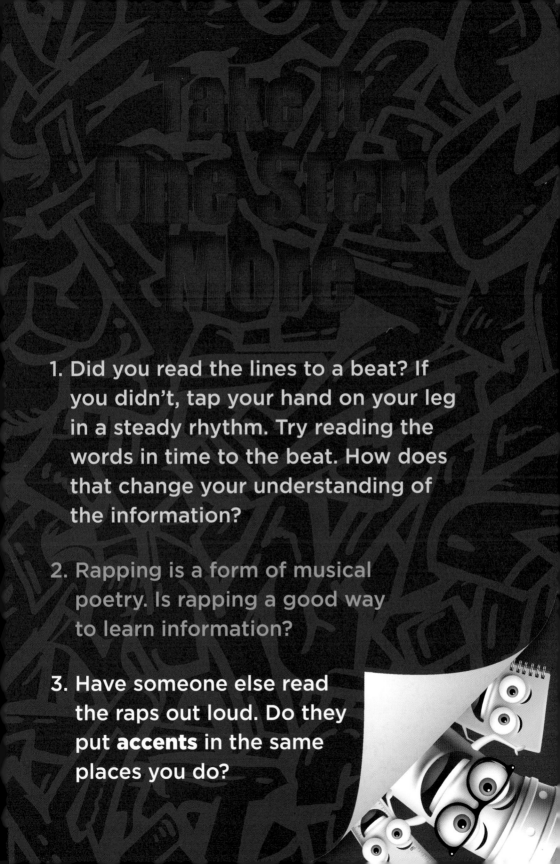

GLOSSARY

accent (AK-sent)—an emphasis put on part of a word

creative arts (kree-AY-tiv ARTS)—activities in art, dance, drama, music, poetry, or other forms of personal expression

cruel (KROOWL)—known to cause pain or suffering

estimate (ES-tuh-mayt)—to determine roughly the size, value, or cost of something

graduation rate (grad-yoo-AY-shun RAYT)—the number of students in a school who complete all the coursework

inspire (in-SPIHR)—to make someone want to do something

turntable (TURHN-tay-buhl)—the part of a record player that turns the record

LEARN MORE

BOOKS

Braun, Eric. *Awesome, Disgusting, Unusual Facts about School.* Our Gross, Awesome World. Mankato, MN: Black Rabbit Books, 2019.

Minden, Cecilia, and Katie Roth. *Writing a Poem.* Write It Right. Ann Arbor, MI: Cherry Lake Publishing, 2019.

Pearson, Yvonne. *12 Great Tips on Writing Poetry.* Great Tips on Writing. Mankato, MN: 12-Story Library, 2017.

WEBSITES

School Poems
www.poetry4kids.com/topic/school/

Writing a Rap – Getting Started
www.youtube.com/watch?v=o6NZoTqWLq4

Bob your head to a beat, and try to get the lines of your raps to fit into the rhythm. If you're rushing your words to make them all fit, chop some out.

Having trouble making a word rhyme? Chances are, there might not be a word that can rhyme it. Pro tip—never try to rhyme the word orange.

Making changes to your raps will only make them better. There's not a rapper alive who gets it right the first time.